The Vale of
Belvoir

The Vale of Belvoir looking north into Leicestershire, Nottinghamshire and Lincolnshire; detail of an engraving printed in 1731. Highlighted are steeples of churches at Newark, Lincoln, Bottesford, Allington, Muston, Long Bennington and Foston. This view from the battlements of Belvoir Castle indicates the compactness of the area; it has changed little during the last two hundred years. Today the bells of the churches of the Vale ring out across the valley as they have done for centuries. A nineteenth-century verse, still quoted, indicates the fondness of the villagers of the Vale of Belvoir for their churches and their bells:

> Colston's cracked panchions,
> Screveton's egg shells,
> Bingham's Tro-rollers,
> and Whatton's merry bells.

The Vale of
Belvoir

TREVOR HICKMAN

Sutton Publishing Limited
Phoenix Mill · Thrupp · Stroud
Gloucestershire · GL5 2BU

First published 1994

Revised Edition 2002

Copyright © Trevor Hickman, 1994, 2002

Title page photograph: Belvoir Castle in 1815.

British Library Cataloguing in Publication Data
A catalogue record for this book is available from the British Library.

ISBN 0-7509-3344-5

Typeset in 11.5/13.5 Photina.
Typesetting and origination by
Sutton Publishing Limited.
Printed and bound in England by
J.H. Haynes & Co. Ltd, Sparkford.

By the Same Author

Around Melton Mowbray in Old Photographs
Melton Mowbray in Old Photographs
East of Leicester in Old Photographs
Around Rutland in Old Photographs
The Melton Mowbray Album
Melton Mowbray to Oakham in Old Photographs

The History of the Melton Mowbray Pork Pie
The History of Stilton Cheese
Leicestershire Memories
The Best of East Leicestershire & Rutland
The Best of Leicester

William Stevenson (1802–91) of Harby, photographed in 1870. William was a waterways administrator for most of his life, working on the Grantham Canal.

Contents

Harby windmill, *c.* 1910.

Introduction

The Vale of Belvoir! – a unique area of England still retaining its individuality, so important in rural areas, the people living in the villages sharing a bond that has been established over many centuries. It has no defined boundaries. No map has ever been published that can accurately state that 'this is the Vale of Belvoir', although the map on page 8 takes a stab at it. The southern borders of the Vale are the Belvoir Ridge and the Harby Hills; in my opinion the eastern boundary follows roughly the line of the old Great North Road; the western boundary roughly the line of the Fosse Way and the high ground west of Long Clawson; the northern boundary (determined by discussion with the people who live and work in the Vale) follows a rough line from Flintham via Sibthorpe to Long Bennington. I have visited every town, village and hamlet listed in this book. Although some villages, such as Foston and Long Bennington, could be considered to be on the very edge, certainly a substantial area of the civil parish of these two villages lies in the Vale.

The Vale of Belvoir is held together to this day by a comradeship that is amazing. It lies in three counties, and there is a friendly rivalry between villages crossing the local council boundaries. The farmers of the Vale use Melton Mowbray cattle market on Tuesdays while many of their wives shop at Newark, two small Midland towns so important to the area. To the south, on the Jurassic escarpment stands Belvoir Castle, seat of the Dukes of Rutland, dominating the landscape viewed from every village in this book. Over the centuries many traders have earned their living in the Vale; in this book are photographs recording the travelling salesmen, men who earned their living selling their produce to the villagers, and in many ways helped to retain the area's uniqueness. All have ceased trading, although agricultural suppliers and contractors still move between the villages, retaining this link. The village carriers of the sixteenth, seventeenth, eighteenth and nineteenth centuries allowed this link to flourish, and on page 148 is a photograph of one of the last carriers to operate in the villages. In every village I visited someone commented on the traders of the past – within living memory we have the Barnes of Long Bennington selling groceries and paraffin, the Rylatts of Flintham selling their excellent bread across the length of the Vale and Payling's, the butchers of Aslockton, who were unique! These along with other traders are part of history now. In these pages I trust I have recorded for future generations this part of the Vale's history. Community spirit and friendly rivalry still exist in this area as they do in most rural areas of our country.

One part of rural life that is 'forever England' is village cricket. In the following pages there are many photographs of village cricket teams and other community sports. The crack of a hard leather ball being hit by a bat made of willow is a marvellously evocative sound, and where better to witness the noble art of playing cricket than on a village green? At Car Colston cricket is played on the largest village green in the whole of England!

Rutland coat of arms. The Manners family of Northumberland, Derbyshire and Leicestershire, Earls of Rutland.

The Vale has always been about farming and today, even though farming methods have changed, it still dominates the life of the area. Now most farms concentrate on arable farming, although there are still a few farmers grazing sheep, supplying milk, rearing fat-stock and farming pigs. A comradeship exists between all farmers – they are careful with their money, wise in their counsel, prudent in purchases and full of advice to strangers, providing unrestrained comments about their neighbours' ability. I remarked to one Vale farmer that in driving around this beautiful area of the Midlands, I was glad that it was still a close-knit farming community, so that even though the crops that are grown had changed, mainly to an intensive system, everyone knew each other and the familiar farming smells were still encountered. He quoted this nineteenth-century verse that even today sums up the friendly, yet abrasive, competitive nature of the people of the Vale:

Hawksworth for money,
Scarrington for wit,
Orston for women,
Thoroton for ....!

Farming was and is the main industry of the Vale, but the industrial revolution came to the area with the opening of the Grantham Canal in 1797, soon followed by the railways. Mining has also played its part while tourism has influenced the economy of the area since the nineteenth century.

This then is my collection, made possible only by the generous help provided by so many people whom I visited and talked to in the Vale of Belvoir during the spring of 1994. I take full responsibility for the presentation of the photographs and for any omissions.

Trevor Hickman

Detail from the Ordnance Survey map of 1824, revised in 1882, showing the suggested perimeter of the Vale of Belvoir.

Section One
Belvoir Castle

A drawing of Belvoir Castle, 1891. The castle is the Leicestershire home of the Dukes of Rutland and the Marquess of Granby.

Belvoir Castle, 1731. This magnificent building was almost completely destroyed by fire on 16 October 1816.

Belvoir Castle, 1789. It was built on the site of earlier castles, the previous one having been demolished in 1649 on the instruction of parliament, as a result of the Civil War.

Belvoir Castle and the dairies, 1834.

The avenue with the dairies of Belvoir Castle, 1915.

Belvoir Castle, 1841.

Belvoir Castle, 1891.

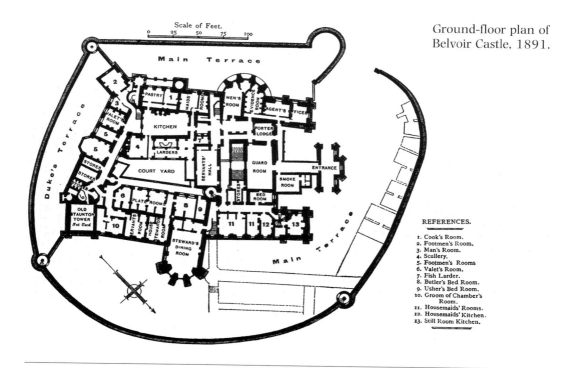

Ground-floor plan of Belvoir Castle, 1891.

REFERENCES.

1. Cook's Room.
2. Footmen's Room.
3. Man's Room.
4. Scullery.
5. Footmen's Rooms
6. Valet's Room.
7. Fish Larder.
8. Butler's Bed Room.
9. Usher's Bed Room.
10. Groom of Chamber's Room.
11. Housemaids' Rooms.
12. Housemaids' Kitchen.
13. Still Room Kitchen.

Belvoir Castle, *c.* 1920. This magnificent 'fairytale' castle sits high on the Belvoir escarpment, an early nineteenth-century reconstruction of a medieval castle.

Belvoir Castle, *c.* 1920. The Revd Sir John Thoroton, commissioned by the Duke of Rutland, saw his magnificent Gothic design completed, despite the interruption of the disastrous fire of 1816.

Entrance to the gardens at Belvoir Castle, 1841.

The Duchess garden at Belvoir Castle, 1925.

The lakes at Belvoir Castle, *c.* 1925.

The hop gardens at Belvoir Castle, *c.* 1906.

The dairy at Belvoir Castle before the First World War. (See page 11.)

The Keeper's Lodge near Belvoir Castle, *c.* 1920.

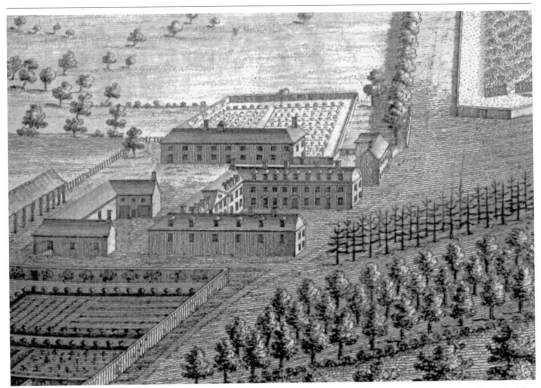

The stables at Belvoir Castle, 1731. These were completed in 1668 to a design by John Webb.

The stables, Belvoir Castle, *c.* 1945.

Guardroom and staircase, Belvoir Castle, 1891.

The guardroom, Belvoir Castle, *c.* 1945.

Interior of the mausoleum at Belvoir
Castle, featuring the Duchess Elizabeth
memorial, 1841.

Staircase in Belvoir Castle, *c.* 1945.

The saloon, Belvoir Castle, *c.* 1945.

The ballroom, Belvoir Castle, *c.* 1945.

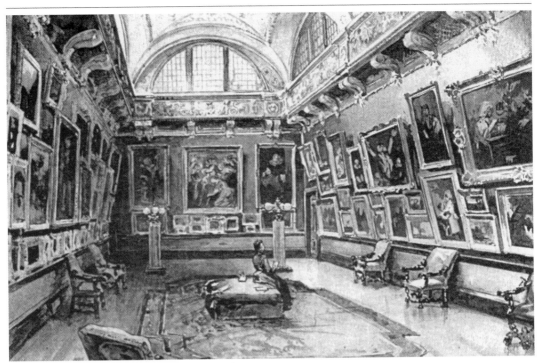

The picture gallery, Belvoir Castle, 1891.

The dining room, Belvoir Castle, c. 1945.

The library, Belvoir Castle, *c.* 1891.

The gallery, Belvoir Castle, *c.* 1945.

John, Marquess of Granby, commanded the British troops during the Seven Years War and in 1766 was made commander-in-chief. He was best known as 'The Generous Granby', as he set up many of his old soldiers as publicans. They then named their public houses after him. (See page 116.)

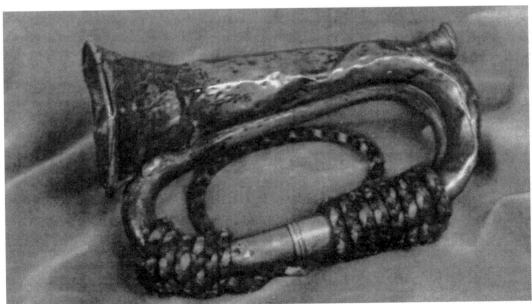

The bugle used by trumpeter William Brittain to sound the charge of the light brigade at Balaklava on 25 October 1854 is now displayed in the Museum of the 17th Lancers at Belvoir Castle.

The 3rd Duke of Rutland, a bust by Nollekens (1737–1823).

Lord Cecil Reginald John Manners, MP for the Melton Division of Leicestershire, 1902. Born in 1868, he was elected MP in 1900 after serving as a war correspondent for the *Morning Star* during the Boer War.

A rent dinner for tenant farmers at Belvoir Castle, 1945. Present are Sir Arthur Curtis of Knipton, the Dowager Duchess and the 10th Duke of Rutland.

Scouts of the 4th Melton Group at Belvoir Castle, on Whit Monday 1941, acting as gate stewards in support of the Dowager Duchess's fund-raising function for the Red Cross. From left to right: Herbert Haines, 'Lal' Southerington, Bob Owens, the 10th Duke of Rutland, Pat Osborn, George Higgins (District Commissioner), John Southerington (ASM), Jack Kelham.

A charabanc outing to Belvoir Castle from Harby and surrounding villages, 1925. Standing in charabanc, left to right: Mary Wright, -?-, Miss Harwood, -?-, Mrs Brown, -?-, -?-, -?-, -?-. Seated in charabanc: -?-, Mrs Watson, Mrs Dora Moles, Mrs Edith Moles, Mrs Mary Pick, Miss Buxton, Queenie Roawingson, Enid Roawingson, -?-, -?-. Standing beside charabanc: -?-. -?-, -?-, Alice Coy. Seated on step: -?-, -?-, Flo Gray, -?-, Mrs Macley, Win Roawingson. Seated on grass: -?-, Ethel Newton, -?-, -?-, Jack Butcher.

The Peacock Hotel, Belvoir, 1906. It is now a private house.

SAVE THE VALE!

Protesters marched through the Vale of Belvoir in the 1970s, objecting to the plan to mine the Vale for coal. In this group are Quentin Lewis, Mike Nichols and Howard Cooper.

A 1977 poster supporting the campaign against the NCB's plans to mine the Vale of Belvoir for coal.

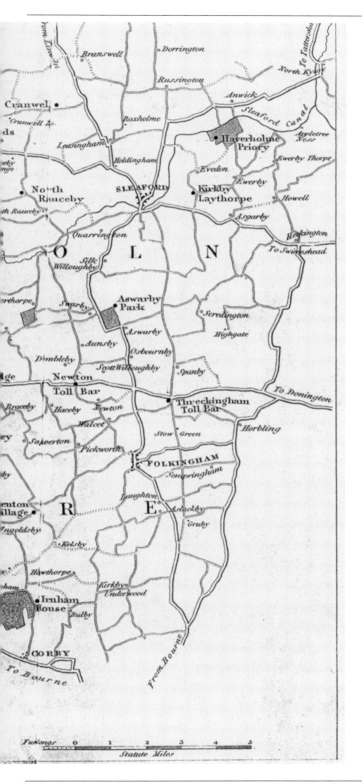

THE BELVOIR HUNT

Map of the Belvoir Hunt country, *c.* 1850.

T. Goosey, Huntsman to the Belvoir Hounds, 1836.

Ben Capell, Huntsman to the Belvoir Hounds, 1900.

The Belvoir Hounds by Sir Francis Grant PRA. (See part two of *Melton Mowbray Album*.)

Fox hunting below Belvoir Castle, 1731.

The Belvoir Hunt: a hunt morning at the kennels by A.J. Munnings RA, *c.* 1930.

The Belvoir Hunt kennels and the Duke of Rutland's Hounds, 1908.

Section Two

Leicestershire

The Vale of Belvoir from the Belvoir escarpment, looking into Nottinghamshire, 1903.

Base of the tower windmill, in use as an agricultural store, 1978.

Ivy Farm, 1920. Dennis Kirk, born in this house in 1920, was a major contributor to this book. Barkestone C. of E. School is in the centre at the end of the road. The headmistress at this time was Mrs R. Gulliver.

Barkestone School, 1904. Back row, left to right: G. Osborn, J. Morris, H. Welch, C. Grass, J. Schofield. Second row: H. Spencer, E. Spencer, T. Welch, E. Poyser, A. Stevens, William Cragg (headmaster). Third row: E. Welch, H. Watchorn, M. Spencer, N. Cross, L. Poyser, R. Welborn. Fourth row: E. Poyser, A. Watchorn, C. Welch, J. Poyser, H. Cross, G. Morris. Front row: H. Spencer, C. Spencer, A. Poyser.

Carting sheaves of corn at Barkestone, 1925. Fred Allen of Redmile is on top of the load, while Dennis Kirk and Tom Bonser Kirk are standing in front of the wagon, waiting for Flower the faithful horse to be led off the field.

The green and ford at Bottesford, 1906.

Base of the market cross and stocks, 1913.

Pensioners at the men's hospital, the Earl of Rutland's Almshouse, 1907.

Advertisement for a local nursery, 1930s.

Market Street, Bottesford, 1905. George Goodson was the licensee of the Bull Hotel.

The Belvoir Hunt passing the Bull Hotel, proprietor George Herbert Goodson, 1945.

Reproduction of a woodcut published in a chapbook in 1620 of the 'Witches of Bottesford'. Joan and Margaret Flower lived with Anne Baker at Bottesford. Joan died, possibly from a heart attack, just before Margaret and Anne were hanged at Lincoln gaol on 11 March 1619.

IN 1608 . HE MARRIED Y: LADY CECILIA HVNGERF: DAVGHT:
TO Y: HON:BLE KNIGHT S:R IOHN TVFTON BY WHOM HE HAD
TWO SONNES, BOTH W:CH DYED IN THEIR INFANCY BY WICKEI
PRACTISE & SORCERYE : IN 1612 . HE WAS MADE LORD
LEIVETENANT OF LINCOLNESH: & AFTER IVSTICE IN EYRE
OF AIL Y: KINGS FORRESTS & CHASES ON Y: NORTH OF
TRENT : IN 1616 . HE WAS MADE KNIGHT OF Y: MOST
NOBLE ORDER OF Y: GARTER : IN Y: YEARE 1616 HE
WAS ONE OF Y: LORDS WHO ATTENDED KING IAMES B:

In Bottesford Church stands the splendid monument to the 6th Duke of Rutland, who died in 1632, and his two wives and children. It bears the inscription reproduced above, which is unique in England.

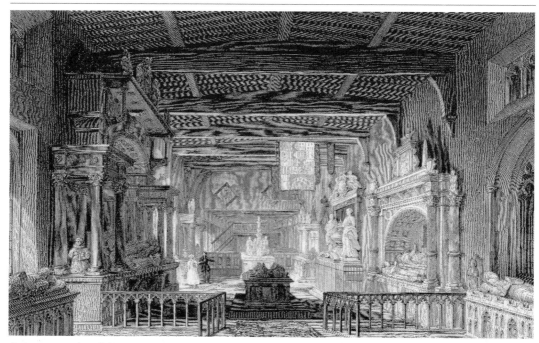

An engraving of the interior of Bottesford Church, looking west from the sanctuary. 1845.

The 6th Duke of Rutland's tomb, 1940s.

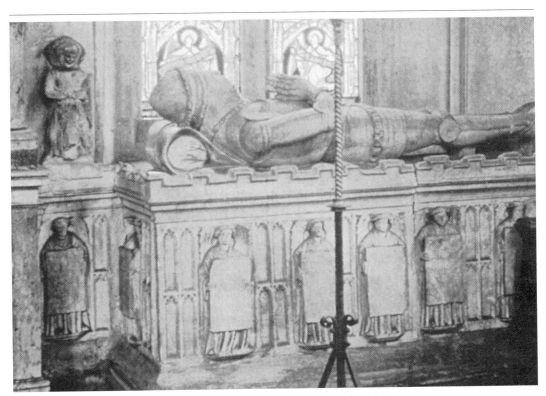

The effigy and monument of John Reas in Bottesford Church, 1940s.

One of the Duke of Rutland's bedesmen dressed in fifteenth-century costume, outside the west door of Bottesford Church, 1907.

Elizabeth Allen's tea gardens near the railway station at Bottesford, just before the First World War.

COMMUNICATION.
(FOR INLAND POSTAGE ONLY)
ALLEN'S TEA GARDENS
and Cyclists' Rest,
BOTTESFORD (near the Station).

REFRESHMENTS AT ANY HOUR.

Apartments.
Parties Catered for.

Postal Adress : A. ALLEN, Devon House, Bottesford.

Advertisement for tourists. Tourism is an essential part of the economy of the Vale of Belvoir. The coming of the railways to the Vale in the late nineteenth century opened up the district, and cycling in the halcyon days before the First World War made it a popular venue. Arriving in the area by train, people bicycled along the peaceful flat lanes of the Vale, visiting the splendid churches and Belvoir Castle, many staying in the apartments at Allen's tea gardens. Tourism still thrives, Belvoir Castle attracting many thousands of visitors. The Vale offers many interesting features, and fine accommodation and apartments are still available locally, especially in the nearby hamlet of Normanton.

Fleming's bridge, *c.* 1910. In the winter of 1606, Dr Samuel Fleming (rector of Bottesford Church 1581–1620) was returning to the village on horseback, and attempted to cross the River Devon in flood. The force of the torrent unseated him and he nearly drowned. At his own expense he had this small packhorse bridge erected.

Albert Street, Bottesford, 1910.

Bottesford School cricket team, 1933. Back row, left to right: George Cloxton, Hugh Miller, David Bolland, Ken Devaril, Len Philpots, Len Henson, Dennis Kirk. Second row: Cyril Taylor, Don Bellamy, Allan Abbott, Ralph Gilbert, Walter Stanley, Aubrey Norris, Harold Speed. Front row: Phil Morley, Jack Kirton.

The Red Lion public house, 1910. Edward Greebury was the licensee.

Bottesford Gas Works, 1948.

Bottesford High Street, 1910.

Scrimshaw's Mill, 1928. The mill ceased working in 1920, when Charles Raithby became too old to work it, and was demolished in 1964.

Floods on Nottingham Road, Bottesford, 1928.

Rutland Arms Hotel, High Street, Bottesford, 1916. John H. Smith was the licensee.

Rutland Arms Hotel, 1960s.

Belvoir Road, Bottesford, 1920.

If you have got the Hump come to BOTTESFORD.

A postcard from Bottesford, 1920s.

Mr and Mrs William Samuel posing in 1920 in front of a gun that was captured during the First World War. It was 'displayed' in the clump of trees at the junction of Devon Lane and the road to Normanton near the ford, which here is in flood. The gun was cut up for scrap metal during the Second World War.

An east coast holiday train northbound to Bottesford, Saturday 1 August 1959. The 4MT, engine no. 43111, is just north of Stathern Junction with the Harby Hills in the background, and is pulling eleven coaches.

Fishing tackle stacked on the
Grantham Canal at Bottesford. This
canal, running from Nottingham to
Grantham, opened in 1797 and was
abandoned in 1936.

William Sutton holding the 48lb pike
he caught in the Grantham Canal
at Bottesford in 1910, assisted by
Mr Charity, who is holding the rod.
This specimen pike did not finish up in
a display case, but was cut up into
steaks and eaten!

EASTHORPE

Three cottages at the junction of Muston Lane and Castle View Road, 1910. They are now one long house called The Corner House.

Guy Lovett, the Easthorpe coal dealer, 1940s.

ROBERT BUXTON,
SHOEING & GENERAL SMITH,
HARBY *(near the School)*.

All kinds of Farm Implements, Hatchets, Hedge-Bills, Garden Tools, &c., made to order.

BICYCLE REPAIRS NEATLY EXECUTED.

ORNAMENTAL PAISADING FOR GRAVES, GARDENS, &C.
MADE ON THE SHORTEST NOTICE.

ALL ORDERS PROMPTLY ATTENDED TO.

Moderate Terms.   Estimates Given.

An advertisement published in the prospectus for Harby Horticultural Gala Exhibition of 1891.

An engraving of the Church of St Mary, Harby, 1792, from a drawing by J. Pridden. Belvoir Castle stands high in the background.

Harby windmill, just before it was 'tail-winded', 1938.

Interior view of Harby windmill, showing the wooden stone nut and iron spur wheel, 1938.

Harby windmill, 1978. During the Second World War this magnificent windmill was partially demolished because it lay on the flight path of planes approaching Langar aerodrome.

Ted Moon on the swing bridge over the Grantham Canal at Harby, 1962.

Harby, viewed across the derelict Grantham Canal, with the steam mill on the left and the base of the windmill on the right, 1978.

Leicester to Colwick goods train passing through Harby and Stathern station, headed by an ex-GNR 0–6–0, no. 64238, 1940s.

The Wesleyan Chapel, 1904. It was built in 1847.

Engraving of the Market Cross at Harby, 1791, from a drawing by J. Pridden. This cross, considered by many historians to have been a Queen Eleanor Cross, has been destroyed. Queen Eleanor died in Nottinghamshire in 1290 and crosses were erected by Edward I, her husband, at each of the stopping places of her cortège on the way to Westminster Abbey.

Harby and Stathern railway station, 1916. Thomas Drury was station-master.

HOSE

An engraving
of Hose Parish
Church, 1791.

Canal bridge at Hose, photographed just before the closure of the Grantham Canal in 1936.

Doubleday Lane, 1930s.

No. 61771 leaving the west end of Hose Tunnel with a Mablethorpe–Leicester Saturday-only train, *c.* 1935.

The school at Hose, 1904.

Hose United Band of Hope, at around the end of the nineteenth century. Back row, left to right: -?-, Edith Huckerby, Nellie Huckerby, Lucy Huckerby, Mabel Huckerby, -?-, -?-, -?-, Maud Hourd, -?-, -?-, -?-, Emily Hourd, Annie Hourd, -?-, Joseph Jesson. Second row: Louie Burnett, -?-, -?-, -?-, -?-, Annie Jesson, -?-, -?-, -?-, Clara Hourd, Frances Jane Wesson, -?-, -?-, -?-, Annie Burnett, -?-, -?-. Front row: Miss Starbuck, -?-, -?-, -?-, -?-, -?-, -?-, John Chester (shopkeeper and local Baptist preacher), -?-, Sarah Corner, Fanny Corner, Mary Anne (Polly) Corner, -?-, -?-, -?-.

Hose cricket club, 1930. Back row, left to right: Harry Hourd, Walter Caunt, Jack Allington, Fred Smith, Cecil Hubbard, George Watson. Front row: Herbert Mabbot, Bob Hallam, Jack Smith, Jack Hunt, Jud Lambert, Arthur Hourd.

Lord Daresbury presenting a cricket competition cup to Walter Caunt, captain of Hose cricket team, 1930.

Members of the Caunt family – Gillian, Sarah, Lucy, Hilda and Edward – on the canal bridge at Hose, 1910.

Hose School, with Mayfield House in the background, 1920. Back row, left to right: W. Harding, F. Baxter, R. Hallam, J. Baxter, Job Baxter, W. Caunt, B. Raynes, L. Stevenson. Second row: D. Marshall, G. Corner, A. Hourd, F. Simpkins, C. Knight, H. Stevenson, I. Simpkins, M. Smith, A. Hourd, C. Knight, E. Caunt, V. Hallam. Third row: M. Baxter, B. Raynes, O. Simpkin, S. Bonsor, O. Hourd, S. Smith, K. Jesson, F. Corner. Front row: F. Harding, A. Jesson, B. Moulds, E. Jesson, G. Preston, T. Caunt, J. Palmer. The headmistress was Mrs Martin.

An engraving of Long Clawson Church, 1791.

The Church of St Remigius, *c.* 1925.

John Moore Swain MRCS Eng., LSA land., of Long Clawson, 1902. He was surgeon and medical officer to the Melton Mowbray Union.

William Buxton (Wesleyan Minister of Long Clawson in 1930), James Bower and Bob Guttridge.

West End, Long Clawson, 1930s.

Main Road, East End, Long Clawson, 1930s.

Mrs Lois Elizabeth Guttridge's grocer's shop in Main Street, 1932.

Long Clawson windmill, 1935.

Wesleyan Methodist Sunday School outing, 1923. This group includes Tom Buxton, the Sunday School superintendent, and Nellie Buxton, while Malcolm King, the bus owner and driver, stands at the back. The bus was built on a second-hand chassis by T. Buxton & Co., of Long Clawson.

Long Clawson School, 1926. This group includes Sam Palmer, Ernest Buxton, Kath Wilford, Bill Buxton, Flo Doubleday, Olive Peers and Alice Wright. Most of the children are wearing boots – these were essential, as many pupils had to walk more than 3 miles to school across fields and muddy lanes.

T. BUXTON & Co.

LONG CLAWSON
AND
CATTLE MARKET
MELTON MOWBRAY

Wheelwrights
—
Motor Body
Builders
—
Joiners

The letterhead of a thriving business that was operating in Long Clawson in the first half of this century.

Employees of T. Buxton & Co., fitting a metal tyre around a wooden cart wheel. Left to right: W. Buxton, T. Buxton snr, G. Buxton, P. Goodson, H. Cooper. When the red hot metal tyre (hoop) is in place water is poured over the rim to contract the metal rapidly, so securing the wooden rims and spokes. This process was known as 'hooping'. (See page 135.)

The Crown and Plough, when Albine Knapp was the licensee, 1904. The thatched cottage has been demolished and the village hall now stands on the site.

The Long Clawson band photographed at Plungar Feast, *c.* 1900. In this group are William Millar, Mr Etterley, Jack Pritchart, George Watchorn, Robert Millar, William Barratt and Jimmy Worthington.

LONG CLAWSON DAIRIES

Staff of the Long Clawson Dairy Ltd, early 1950s. Back row, left to right: M. Thorn, D. Hourd, F. Lambert, C. Pym, E. Keightley, G. Crooks. Second row: Mrs B. MacDonough, Mrs Farrington, -?-, Mrs Morley jnr, Mrs Darby, Miss H. Hallam, Mrs C. Smith, Mrs Hall, Mrs Morley, Mrs Hourd, Mrs P. Pagett, Mr Tom Wiles. Front row: Mrs Stapleforth, -?-, -?-, Mrs Merry, Mrs P. Rawlings, Mrs Richardson. The lorry driver is Steve Wass. Mrs Merry is holding the Mathew Skailes Challenge Cup for the best blue-veined cheese produced in Britain.

The 'young' Stiltons are removed from the moulds before they are 'bandaged', which allows them to sweat, 1950. Left to right: Miss H. Hallam, Mrs Richardson, Mrs Hall.

MUSTON

Engraving of the Church of St John the Baptist, 1789.

The poet George Crabbe was appointed rector of Muston Church in 1789. This was not a happy time for him, as he had continuous disagreements with his dissenting parishioners. Crabbe enjoyed the company of many famous people, including Sir Joshua Reynolds and Samuel Johnson, and he had the patronage of the Duke of Rutland. While at Muston he wrote these lines in *The Borough*, which was published in 1810:

> Seek then thy garden's shrubbery bound, and look,
> As it steals by, upon the bordering brook;
> That winding streamlet, limpid, lingering slow,
> Where the reeds whisper when the zephyrs blow;
> Where in the midst, upon a throne of green,
> Sits the large lily as the water's queen;
> And makes the current, forced awhile to stay,
> Murmur and bubble as it shoots away.

The main road looking north, with Winthorpe House on the right and Three Shires Farm on the left, 1910.

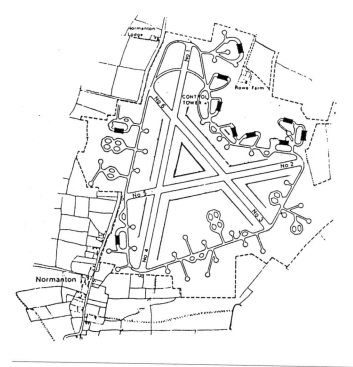

A plan of the hamlet of Normanton, 1944. It shows the extensive aerodrome that dominated the area during the Second World War.

Ernest, Leonard and Wilf Barnes with the brood mare at Willow Farm, Normanton, *c.* 1915.

The main road looking north, with Rose Cottage on the right and the barn and dovecote on the left, 1910.

PLUNGAR

Granby Lane, Plungar, 1910.

John Kirk at Pasture Farm, 1932.

The Church of St Helen, 1791. This engraving is from a drawing by J. Pridden.

Skaters on the Grantham Canal at Plungar, 1920. Left to right: -?-, -?-, Gwen Wilford, Billy Welbourn, Joy Wilford, Joe Pell, Ada Moulds, Frank Wilford, Jean Pell, Mary Pell, -?-, Geoff Pell, -?-, -?-.

Tom Bonser Kirk cutting wheat with a horse-drawn binder at Poplar Farm, 1930. The horses are (left to right) Bonny, Captain and Blossom.

Bonny between the shafts drawing a wagon load of sheaves of wheat at Poplar Farm, 1935. Fred Allen is on top of the load. Left to right: Tom Bonser Kirk, Frank Kirk, Dennis Kirk, Dick Skelham.

A group of lads on Plungar swing bridge on the Grantham Canal, 1924. Left to right: Clifford Worthington, Reg Caunt, Geoff Kirk, Frank Bass.

Haystacks at Pasture Farm, Plungar, photographed from Chapel Street, 1937.

An engraving of the Church of St Peter, 1789.

Church Lane with Valley Farm House on the left, 1910.

Wesleyan Chapel Sunday School anniversary, 1921. Members of the congregation have gathered outside the post office, run by Harold Carlile.

In 1925 the Rectory was the home of the Revd Stephen Parkinson BA, of Corpus Christi College, Cambridge. In the foreground runs the Grantham Canal. The photographer was standing near the spillway to the River Grimmer, which passes under the canal at this point.

A class J6 engine is pulling the evening train from Grantham to Leicester, and is standing in the ornate railway station at Redmile, *c.* 1940. The Dukes of Rutland had a private waiting room at the station.

Redmile Church photographed from across the Grantham Canal and over the embankment protecting the village. It is an idyllic scene from before the First World War.

A class K2 engine is pulling the holiday train bound for the east coast, and passing through the derelict site of the recently demolished Redmile railway station, Saturday 1 August 1959.

Redmile football club, 1920–1. Back row, left to right: F. Daley, G.W. Marriott, G. Hutchinson. Second row: T.W. Clower, H. Tinkler, A. Clamp, H. Munks, W. Day, F. Tolladay, A. King. Third row: B. Pacey, B. Morley, W.B. Morley, H. Chandler, W. Pegg. Front row: W. Cox, W. Pacey, W. Morley. B. Morley later played for Nottingham Forest FC.

Redmile windmill, 1930.

The parish church of St Guthlac, 1791.

Stathern post office, 1925. Mrs Mary Barke was the postmistress.

St Guthlac viewed from Church Lane, 1906. The vicar was the Revd John William Taylor MA, JP.

Council houses, Stathern, built on the junction of Blacksmith's End and Birds Lane, *c.* 1950. Anvil House stands in the distance.

Stathern tower windmill, *c.* 1895. John and George Braithwaite's lace-making factory is on the right.

A class B1 engine pulling the Skegness to Leicester train past Stathern Junction signal box, late 1940s.

British Rail ironstone sidings at Stathern with the lorry tippler in the background, 1966.

Mr Stead and Mr Swingler outside their blacksmith's shop, *c.* 1910.

The village of Stathern from Tofts Hill, *c.* 1910.

Amadine Booth with her daughter at the entrance to her cottage that stood off the green at Stathern, 1908. The cottage has since been demolished.

A Great Northern class K2 engine pulls the holiday special train just leaving Stathern Junction on Bank Holiday Monday, 3 August 1959. This train ran from Belgrave Road Station, Leicester, via Melton Mowbray to the east coast.

A class B1 engine heads a northbound train with empty ironstone wagons, taking the line to Saxondale Junction and on to Colwick, Saturday 22 July 1961. The Harby Hills are in the background.

Section Three
Nottinghamshire

The Vale of Belvoir from the Harby Hills, looking into Nottinghamshire, 1940s.

ALVERTON

Staunton School at Alverton, coronation day, 1937. Left to right: Eric Fenton, Jeff Cox, Donald Murdock, David Merrin, Dorothy Forth, -?-, Margaret Stevenson, George Forth, Betty Lane, Joan Bramford, Les Longdon, Stan Gladders, Willy Miller, Raymond Cragg, Wally Miller.

Jeff Burton and Dennis Patchett on the tractor, with Billy Baker on the binder, cutting and binding corn into sheaves, summer 1947.

John Odell shearing sheep, 1979. Jeff Burton is carrying the rolled fleece.

Jeff Burton and Jack Lambert resting after loading 18-stone bags of wheat on to a trailer.

At Newark Show, Billy Baker was presented with a long service medal for working with the Burton family of Alverton for over forty years.

ASLOCKTON

George Potter posing in the doorway of his post office and shop, 1926. Eric Barker is holding his bicycle. The child hiding behind the basket is Lewis Smith.

The nineteenth-century tower of St Thomas's Church, Aslockton, *c.* 1906.

Thomas Cranmer, Archbishop of Canterbury, was born at Aslockton in 1489. He supported Henry VIII's claim to be the supreme head of the Church of England. Cranmer was burned at the stake for heresy during Queen Mary's reign, in 1556, at Oxford.

Aslockton post mill, *c*. 1880.

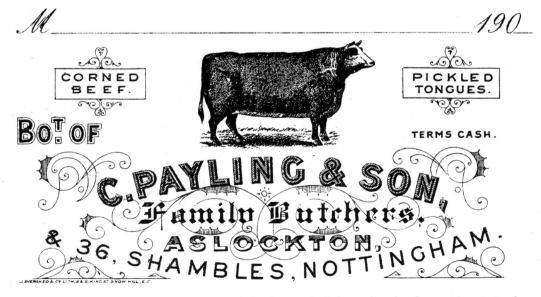

Payling's butchering business is part of the history of the Vale of Belvoir. Mrs C. Payling carried on the business after her husband died, trading out of Aslockton and the Shambles in Nottingham, where on Saturday afternoons the week's 'leftovers' were sold cheaply to the poor. A formidable woman, when a beast was being pole-axed in the slaughter house, she would stand in the doorway and deliver the *coup de grâce* with a single rifle shot if the unfortunate animal did not succumb to the first terrible blow.

Floods in Aslockton, Bank Holiday Monday, 8 August 1922. Bert Baxter, a local butcher and church organist, is attempting to clean out the drains with a garden rake.

Aslockton station, *c.* 1920. Left to right: Jack Guy, Fred Mooney, -?-, Mr Ward (station-master), Mr Bickerstaff (clerk).

BARNSTONE

The Institute, Barnstone, *c.* 1920.

The Walnuts, Barnstone, 1915. Left to right: Daisy, Mabel, 'Bunny' Harwood.

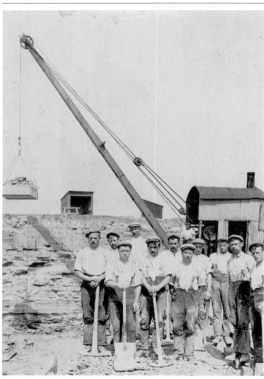

Barnstone cement works, *c.* 1930. This group of quarrymen, standing in front of a steam-driven crane, includes 'Gummy' Slater, Jack Wheatman, Billy Pepper, George Freeman, Harry Bollands, S. Wade and H. Towle.

The remains of the same crane before it was cut up for scrap, November 1969.

Barnstone station looking north towards Bingham Road and Saxondale Junction, August 1959. By this time the station was closed to passenger services.

Barnstone cement works, 1910. The men are sorting stone to be fed into the crushers to make ground or lump lime.

The Belvoir Hunt at Barnstone cement works, 21 February 1953. Left to right: Jim Webster (first whip), Col. Hanbury (MFH), George Tong.

Nottingham Forest football club won the FA Cup in 1959. Here the cup is on display at Barnstone Social Club. Left to right: L. Watson, F. Chambers (director, Nottingham Forest FC), J. Sail, J. Wood (director, Nottingham Forest FC), D. Jackson.

Interior of the joiner's shop at Barnstone cement works, before the First World War.

Station Street, Bingham, *c.* 1916.

Cherry Street, Bingham, *c.* 1950.

Bingham railway station, *c*. 1920.

The Rectory, Bingham, 1904. Lily Langtry was a frequent visitor to this house.

Church of St Mary and All Saints, Bingham, 1904.

The interior of Bingham Church, 1909.

An engraving of Queen Victoria as a young woman. On 4 December 1843 Queen Victoria visited Bingham. The streets were decorated with flags and lined by cheering crowds, and the Queen's coach was escorted by the 6th Enniskillen Dragoons under the command of Colonel Moore, across the Vale of Belvoir to Belvoir Castle.

An engraving of Prince Albert, who accompanied the Queen on her visit to Bingham in 1843.

Fairfield Street, Bingham, 1916.

Market Place, with the steeple-roofed butter cross, 1906.

Nicholson's decorated carrier's cart, hired by the Blood family who lived at The Crown public house, Market Place, *c.* 1920.

Market Place, Bingham, 1960s.

This was possibly the very first car to be driven along the streets of Bingham.

A motor-cyclist outside Walker's motor engineers, 1923.

CAR COLSTON

Flinders Cottage viewed from the 'Big Green' before the First World War. The village greens at Car Colston are the largest in Britain, covering over 20 acres.

Cutting corn at Car Colston, 1932. Jack Gilbert is on the binder, while Jackie Marriot (assisted by Bert Fretwell) is threading the binder twine.

Composite drawing by D.I. Herbert of Thoroton's house and garden, based on a print by J. Throsby, 1797. Old Hall was the home of Dr Robert Thoroton, the famous seventeenth-century Nottinghamshire historian.

Old Hall from the church tower, showing the original walled garden, 1975.

A Car Colston football team at the cricket pavilion on the 'Big Green', 1974. Back row, left to right: Robin Renshaw, -?-, -?-, George Willis, David Grayson, David Penson, David Rose, -?-. Front row: Peter Willis, Carman Hardy, John Appleby, John Gilbert, -?-.

William Wilkinson carting water from 'Little Green' at Car Colston, during the drought of 1933.

Church Gate, with the Church of St John the Divine standing high to the left, 1910.

Junction of Church Gate and Harby Lane, *c.* 1916.

The ruined church tower of St Mary's stands in the fields of Colston Bassett. The le Marchants built the present church in the nineteenth century, allowing this church to fall into ruins.

The remains of the manor house built by Francis and Margaret Hacker. The inscription on the chimney stack reads 'F.H.M.H. 1625'. Their eldest son, Colonel Francis Hacker, fought for Cromwell during the Civil War; he was declared a traitor after the restoration and was hanged at Tyburn in 1660. The two younger sons fought for Charles I. Thomas was killed at Colston Bassett in a skirmish with Roundhead troops, but Rowland survived and Charles II granted him the right to claim the estate forfeited by his elder brother.

Elton Rectory, 1914. This house stands on the junction of the road to Orston and the main Nottingham to Grantham road.

The Manor House, Elton, before the First World War. It was demolished in the 1930s.

FLAWBOROUGH

Mr J.A. Drury, the postman from Staunton, handing the mail to Annie Beet, maid at Flawborough Hall, 1936.

Eric Pell riding a hunter on the main road at Flawborough, 1929. The thatched farmhouse at the side of the road in the background has since been demolished.

Flintham main street, 1908. William Holder Rylatt sits in his bread cart under the tree, opposite the general stores run by the Rylatt family.

William Archibald Rylatt filling the bread baskets that each held six loaves from the bread cart on Car Colston village green, 1950. Daisy is tied to the signpost: if not tethered, and left unattended, she would calmly trot back home to Flintham.

William Holder Rylatt, master baker of Flintham, 1960. The Rylatt family moved to Flintham from Beckingham in 1893, setting up their baking business which traded throughout the Vale of Belvoir. (See page 118.) The Rylatts became a legend in their own lifetimes, baking superb bread and also excelling on the cricket pitches throughout the Vale. They ceased baking because they were overwhelmed by Common Market bureaucracy, but their bakehouse still stands in the village.

GRANBY

Walker & Sons, saddlers, Granby.

Alfred Watson, publican, outside the Marquis of Granby public house, 1925.

Main Street, Granby, 1925.

Arthur Dalby chain harrowing at Granby, *c.* 1935.

Joe Spence 'muck carting' with Brisk, before the Second World War.

Rylatts' bread cart from Flintham with Mr Renson to the left of the cart, 1908. Charlie and Kath Penson are standing on the highway.

Main Street, Hawksworth, before the First World War. A wheat-straw stack made up of sheaves waiting to be threshed stands in front of a haystack.

George Dable and Fred Hopkinson driving sheep down Town Street, *c.* 1930.

Wagon loads of gypsum outside the crusher house at Kilvington quarries, 1950s.

Drag-line working the open-cast gypsum quarries, *c.* 1950.

LANGAR

The Church of England School with pupils posing outside, January 1967.

Langar School, 1898. Mabel Harwood is first from the left on the back row, Daisy Harwood is sixth from the left on the second row, and Manny Harwood is first from the left on the front row.

The village gathering at Miss Bayley's wedding to Mr Percy Haskingson at Langar Hall, 1904.

Admiral of the Fleet Earl Howe KG (1726–99) was victorious over the French on the 'Glorious First of June' when he captured seven ships of the line (the finest French ships) off Ushant. One of the Langar Howes, he is buried in the parish church.

Langar, 1936. The village public house and post office are situated opposite this row of cottages.

The author Samuel Butler lived at the rectory at Langar where he was born in 1834; he died in 1902. He wrote a number of books that generated considerable interest in the literary world, none more so than *Erewhon*. This controversial phallic design by Blair Hughes-Stanton, on the Gregynog Press edition, caused an outcry when it was released in 1932.

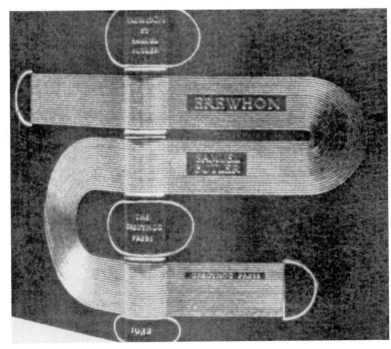

Langar Boys' Brigade, 1910. Third from the left on the front row stands Dalton James, only son of Mr John James, publican at The Unicorn. Dalton died of consumption at the age of eighteen.

The cover of *Picture Post*, May 1943. Jack Hyde flew out of Langar aerodrome where this photograph was taken. 207 Squadron, RAF, was based here from 1942 to 1943.

ORSTON

Chapel Street, Orston, 1936. The post office, run by Mrs Walker, is on the left, with
Scotney's builders' yard on the right.

Orston windmill was demolished in 1923 by
Wakes & Lamb of Newark. Parts were then
sent to New Zealand, where they were
incorporated into Partington's windmill,
Auckland, which in turn was demolished
in 1950.

Harvesting hay at Orston Grange, 1930. Fred Chapell and friend are on top of the wagon, stacking the hay.

Windpump, Orston Grange, *c.* 1938. This type of pump was in widespread use throughout the Vale until the Second World War. With the laying of water mains, they fell into disrepair, through neglect.

SCARRINGTON

Scarrington School (juniors), 1932. Back row, left to right: Dennis Pritchett, Nathian Davey, John Mee, Ted Muncaster, Ken Briggs, Rod Arnett, Harold Sills, Stan Smith. Second row: Lil Yates, Pat Seves, May Allen, Olive Kirkland, Gladys Carr, Ivy Nash, Beryl Birkin, Joyce Worley, Joan Baker. Front row: Dorothy Gastalo, Edna Pritchett, Hazel Baker, Betty Worley, Ruth Towle, Tom Kirkland, Ella Morrison, Edith Arnott, Leslie Sills, Peter Morrison.

Thatched cottages built of mud cob and mud stud at Little Lunnon, Scarrington, c. 1900.

Thatched cottage falling into disrepair, 1906. This enclave of cottages was built on the outskirts of the village of Scarrington to house the poor of the area. All the cottages at Little Lunnon were pulled down during the 1920s and 1930s.

The Scarrington blacksmith's famous pile of cast-off horseshoes. In 1970 the village blacksmith George Flinders sold this unique stack of horseshoes to a visiting American tourist. The district council was not amused and immediately put a preservation order on the pile – it now has a Grade II listing.

Screveton Church, 1980. Mr Pole-Karew and Mrs Joan Raspin standing on top of the tower at the dedication of the new stairs in the tower.

William Wilkinson mowing hay at The Poplars, Screveton, 1936.

Stacking hay at The Poplars, 1937. Lawrence Widdowson and Irvine Wilkinson are on top of the stack. Edith Wilkinson, with her grandson John, is standing next to William Wilkinson, who is lifting more hay on to the stack.

SHELTON

Gersham Simpson on an unusual swathe turner turning hay at Shelton, *c.* 1920.

B Company, 11th (Newark) Battalion, Nottinghamshire Home Guard at Shelton Park, November 1944. In this photograph are Fred Scotney, John Shepard, Maxwell Barnes, Sam Bellamy, Tony Burton, Bill Charlton, George Bellamy, Bill Cragg, Jim Drury, Joe Henderson, Harry Sentance, Major Birch, Captain Brown, Captain Pell, Stan Shelton, Charles Thurman, Bert Cragg, Frank Cragg and Bill Pell.

SIBTHORPE

Dovecote at Sibthorpe, *c.* 1938. Maggie Burton with her husband Leslie, the then owner of the dovecote, with Tommy Wright and Vera Burton. The dovecote is now owned by Nottinghamshire County Council.

Interior of the dovecote. This is all that remains of a fine monastic college founded and endowed by Thomas de Sibthorpe in 1372. The terrible famine that Nottinghamshire experienced in 1316 no doubt encouraged the monks to build this very large dovecote, which contained about 1,260 nesting holes, to help to ensure adequate supplies of food during any further trouble. The fat squabs no doubt complemented the carp raised in the nearby ponds, fed with water from the adjacent 'Car Dyke'.

STAUNTON

Staunton Hall, the home of the Staunton family for over 900 years, 1906. The Stauntons were royalists in the Civil War. The central part of the Elizabethan hall survives between Georgian extensions. Marks of the attack by Roundhead soldiers in 1645 are still apparent, including two cannonball holes in the front door.

Entrance to the library in Staunton Hall, 1889. The 1652 painting of Mrs Staunton, the wife of Colonel William Staunton, still hangs above the door.

The Staunton Arms public house, *c.* 1910. Corner Farm is on the left, Elms Farm on the right.

George Drury, chauffeur, with James Drury and family outside the post office, Staunton, 1921.

Carol Drury assisting her husband Tom to fix a metal rim around a wooden wheel, 1973. The Drurys of Staunton have been wheelwrights for four generations. Tom Drury still practises his craft. Heat for expanding the metal rim for 'hooping' is now provided by burning discarded rubber tyres! (See page 68.)

Cutting fence rails at the Drurys wheelwright's yard, c. 1910. The five people at the saw bench with the freshly cut rails are, left to right: William Drury, Ernest Drury, James Drury, James Arthur Drury, John Drury.

A bicycling party at Staunton Hall, 1905. In this photograph is Harvey Staunton who played for Nottinghamshire County Cricket Club before the First World War.

Colonel William Staunton was with Charles I when he raised the standard at Nottingham in August 1642. He fought at Edgehill and Brentford. In 1643 he raised a regiment of 1,200 foot soldiers who endured the siege of Newark, until the surrender of the town to the Roundheads in 1646.

Handbell ringers at Staunton, 1936. Back row, left to right: Daisy Bellamy, Edith Merchant. Front row: Pansy Drury, Annie Pincheon, Mary Drury.

John Lee of Sutton driving his pony and trap, 1938. Topsy is between the shafts.

Allen Humphrey and his sister Ethel in the doorway of Willow Cottage, Sutton, *c.* 1920.

William Stevenson gathering sheaves of wheat for stooking at Holly Farm, 1940.

The last straw burn at Thoroton, 1992. The end of an era, now that stubble burning in open fields is prohibited.

The memorial stone on the grave of Ethel Gordon Fenwick SRN in Thoroton churchyard. Ethel was the very first state registered nurse and is considered to be the founder of the modern nursing profession.

Thatched dovecote at Thoroton. It is still standing.

Bill and Jim Stevenson at Holly Farm with their mother, *c.* 1920.

Charity fund-raising function organized by Lady Graham (centre) at Wiverton Hall, near Tithby, *c.* 1960.

The charred and burnt carcasses of cows that had been chained in their stalls when a disastrous barn fire broke out at Smite Hall Farm near Tithby, 1914.

WHATTON

The Griffin's Head public house, *c.* 1916.

Whatton and Aslockton cricket club, 1954. Back row, left to right: Malcolm Kirk (scorer), Bill Payling, Bill Lambert, Les Pritchett, Ted Fox (captain), Frank Pritchett, Len Payling, Don Codling. Front row: Jack Kettle (umpire), John Avey, John Piper, Lyn Worley, Arthur Pritchett.

Whatton Lodge was struck by lightning, 20 March 1904.

Whatton Mill, 1900. Mr Fred Houghton, miller, is standing in the doorway with Mr Carter and his son Charles.

Yard and cottage behind Gables Farm off Church Street, 1893. Mrs Summerfield stands in the doorway with her daughter near the bucket. This cottage has now been demolished.

Section Four

Lincolnshire

The Vale of Belvoir from Belvoir Castle, looking into Lincolnshire, 1940s.

Allington Rectory, the home of the Revd William Handcock Rowlands LD of Lampeter College, 1919.

The main street, 1909. The stables are on the left; in the centre is the Welby Arms public house, licensee William Frederick Muxlow; and to the right stands Corner House.

The Red House, home of James Douglas Groves, and the village green, 1909.

The salt well on the Sedgebrook to Allington road. According to Basil Peacock, who had farmed the adjacent land, this well is fed from a fast flowing underground stream that never dries up, no matter how severe the drought. Originally an open well, it was later fitted with a hand pump, but now the water flows, unwanted, into the nearby stream.

FOSTON

The post office on the Newark Hill at the junction with Church Street, 1909. Stephen Speed was the postmaster.

Main Street, Foston, 1918. Western House is on the left.

The Black Horse public house, with the Church of St Peter in the background, 1950.

William Burton's farmyard at Foston, 1910. All these farm buildings have now been demolished.

Mrs Rebecca Dickinson, registered carrier, is holding the horse's head, while her two sons are sitting inside the carrier's cart, 1909. The cart is loaded with produce to deliver to the local market for the villagers of Foston and the surrounding district. Mrs Dickinson attended the markets at Newark on Wednesdays and Grantham on Saturdays.

Interior of a dovecote at Foston. This medieval structure, constructed of mud bound together with straw and small pebbles, was destroyed when the A1 bypass was built at Foston in 1960.

LONG BENNINGTON

The Great North Road, Long Bennington, 1907. On the right stands the Royal Oak public house, Joseph Pearson licensee, with the White Swan public house a few yards further down the road, licensee William Porter Brutnell.

Walter Barnes by his horse before moving off with his travelling shop to trade in the Vale of Belvoir, *c*. 1920. Walter Barnes was also the local carrier attending Newark market on Wednesdays and Fridays, Grantham on Saturdays.

VALUABLE
LIVE & DEAD STOCK.

TO BE SOLD BY

Auction,

BY S. AND J. RIDGE,

On the Premises

At Bennington Lodge Farm,

(FIVE MILES FROM NEWARK,)

On *THURSDAY*, the 11th Day of *DECEMBER*, 1828,

THE WHOLE OF THE

LIVE STOCK,

AND

FARMING UTENSILS,

IN THE FOLLOWING LOTS, VIZ.

1 Six in-lambed ewes	34 Ditto ditto	67 Scuffler	102 Ditto
2 Six ditto	35 Spotted calf	68 Land roller	103 Scythe
3 Six ditto	36 Red calf	69 Grindstone	104 Six hand forks
4 Six ditto	37 White do.	70 Turnip drill	105 Two pitch forks
5 Six ditto	38 A three-year-old draught	71 Straw cutter	106 Two teaming ditto
6 Six ditto	mare	72 Bean mill	107 Two shovels
7 Six ditto	39 A five year-old ditto	73 Winnowing machine	108 Three manure forks
8 Seven ditto	40 An in-foal black draught	74 Strike and roller	109 Four hand rakes
9 Five culled ewes	mare	75 Corn screen	100 Swathe rake
10 Six heder lambs	41 Ditto ditto	76 Pitch-pot and brand	111 Grub axe
11 Six ditto	42 Black barren ditto	77 Three oak beast cribs	112 Hill hoe
12 Six ditto	43 Ditto ditto	78 Three ditto	113 Two picks
13 Six sheder lambs	44 Black cart foal	79 Twelve fence trays	114 Stonepit iron bar
14 Six ditto		80 Twelve ditto	115 Three stonepit hammers
15 Six ditto	45 to 51 Tackle complete for 6	81 Twelve ditto	116 Six weed hooks
16 An in-calved cow	horses	82 Twelve ditto	117 Six hoes
17 Ditto ditto	52 Narrow-wheeled waggon,	83 Twelve ditto	118 Iron stove
18 A three-year-old red steer	with sideboards & shelvings	84 Twelve ditto	119 Four waggon chains
19 A three-year-old black-pol-	53 Do. with shelvings	85 A 38 stove ladder	120 Four gate heads
led ditto	54 Broad-wheeled cart and	86 A 25 ditto ditto	121 Six ditto
20 Two-year-old dun heifer	shelvings	87 A 24 ditto ditto	122 Four heads and bars, for a
21 Two-year-old red ditto	55 Ditto with sideboards	88 Ladder	tumbril
22 Two-year-old do. do.	56 A narrow-wheeled cart with	89 Ditto	123 Sundry tray bars
23 Two-year-old black do.	boards	90 Large stone trough	124 Twelve gate bars
24 Two-year-old spotted steer	57 Plough and swingletree	91 Three pig troughs	125 Twelve ditto
25 Two-year-old black do.	58 Ditto	92 Twelve sack bags	126 Twelve ditto
26 Two-year-old black-polled	59 Ditto	93 Twelve ditto	127 Thirty-six tray bars
ditto	60 Ditto	94 Twelve ditto	128 About 36 feet of oak timber
27 Yearling spotted heifer		95 Pig cratch	129 Four sheep cribs
28 ——— white heifer	61 Two pair of plough gears	96 Mash tub	130 Foal crib
29 Yearling black-polled ditto	62 Set of jingle harrows	97 Gathering tub	131 Lumber
30 ——— red steer	63 Pair of one-horse harrows	98 Small tub	132 Two broad wheels
31 ——— white ditto	64 Ditto	99 Ale barrel	133 One narrow ditto
32 ———red and white ditto	65 Ditto	100 Ditto	
33 Red and white calf	66 Pair of seed harrows	101 Ditto	

THE SALE TO COMMENCE AT TEN O'CLOCK.

S. AND J. RIDGE, PRINTERS, NEWARK.

A farm sale poster, 1828.

Tommy Peatman, postman, in the middle of the Great North Road near William Crabtree's grocer's shop and bakehouse, 1908. Crabtree's is now Potts Stores.

This photograph, taken in the 1930s, shows the garage that stood on the side of the Great North Road which was demolished when the Long Bennington bypass was built in the 1960s. Two bungalows now occupy this site opposite the school.

Long Bennington windmill in the 1920s, just before it was demolished. George Rowbotham was miller in 1909.

The sluice at the water mill on the River Witham, Westborough Road, 1935. Gash & Sons were running this mill in 1925. It is still a mill, although no longer powered by water, and processes specialist horse feed.

SEDGEBROOK

A Grantham-bound class J6 pulls into Sedgebrook station, late 1950s.

The tower leading to the medieval gallery high up in the chancel of the Church of St Lawrence. This church stands near the site of the small monastery of Newbo, and some structures inside this small church are indicative of monastic influence.

Woolsthorpe Band parading down the Main Street during Woolsthorpe Feast, August 1920. Ivy Cottage is on the right.

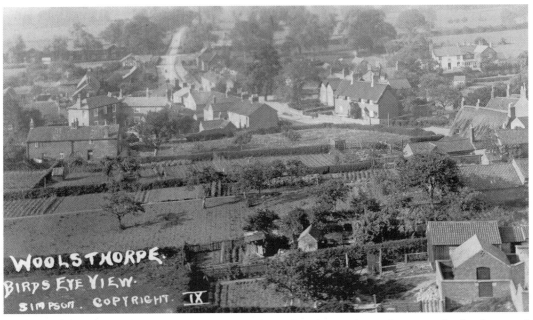

Woolsthorpe from the church tower, 1919. The Belvoir Hunt kennels are in the background to the left. The Chequers Inn is to the right; the licensee was William Clark.

The Belvoir Hunt stables, Belvoir Road, Woolsthorpe, 1922.

Woolsthorpe photographed from the fields, with Belvoir Castle high in the background, c. 1920.

Woolsthorpe from the pastures, *c.* 1920.

The Church of St James, 1919. The vicar was the Revd Robert Harry Bagnall of St John's College, Oxford. This church was built at the expense of the Duke of Rutland to a design by G.G. Place, on the site of St Mary's chapel of ease. It was completed in 1893.

The Chequers Inn public house, 1950s.

An engraving of a drawing, made by the Revd W. Peters in 1792, of the ruins of St James's Church, which stood on the road to Harston. It was destroyed in 1645 by Cromwellian troops who had used it as their barracks while besieging Belvoir Castle, standing high in the background. The grass-covered mounds in the graveyard are the only evidence left.

Phillips' brewery cart of Stamford leaving the lane to the Chequers Inn, opposite Worthington Lane, after delivering mineral water, 1919.

Thatched cottages before the disastrous fire, 1904. Now re-roofed with tiles, they are numbered 1, 2, 3 and 4 Main Street.

Acknowledgements

Putting together this collection of photographs has been made possible only through the kind co-operation of very many people. The author has a small collection of Vale of Belvoir photographs that formed the basis of this selection. Most of the photographs published in this book have been provided by people who still live and work in this delightful area of England, or have an interest in the district. The author's grateful thanks are recorded to:

Bill Wilkinson • Rigby Graham • Neville Scarborough • Michael Neale William
Buxton • Dennis Kirk • Nigel Moon • Elizabeth Staunton
W.B. Moore • Dorothy Beadham • Dorothy Watchorn • Ken Beeby
Margaret Ogden • Esther Sheardown • Tom Drury • Betty Wadkin
Cherry Bishop • Jack Spence • Len Watson • Richard Fenn • Robert H. Brown
William A. Rylatt • Henry Carrington • Jeffrey Burton • William Pell
Tony Burton • Kathleen Simpson • Edwin Fox • Len Payling
Janet Greasley • Andy Wiles.

Permission has been granted to reproduce all the photographs in this book where copyright rights are retained. Should this not be the case concerning some photographs, Trevor Hickman offers his sincere apologies for reproducing them without permission and will make an acknowledgement in future editions. Thanks are also due to all those people in so many villages that the author visited in the spring of 1994 who willingly offered help and advice. Finally thanks are due to Pat Peters for neatly typing the text for the publisher's use.

List of Places & Features